Immortal PRAISE

13 CREATIVE ARRANGEMENTS FOR ORGAN

Moderate

BY TERRY BALDRIDGE

CONTENTS

For Carlene Neihart

O God, Our Help in Ages Past

St. ANNE

Sw. Full
Gt. Full
Ped. Full

WILLIAM CROFT
Arranged by Terry L. Baldridge

Gt. (Principal 8' & 4')
Sw. (Strings 8' & 4')
Bourdon 16' & 8'

rit.
legato
Gt.
detached

legato
rit.
Melody
Full with solo reeds

Full

How Firm a Foundation

FOUNDATION

Sw. Trumpet 8'
Gt. Principal 8'
Ped. Diapason 16' & 8'

Traditional American Melody
Arranged by Terry L. Baldridge

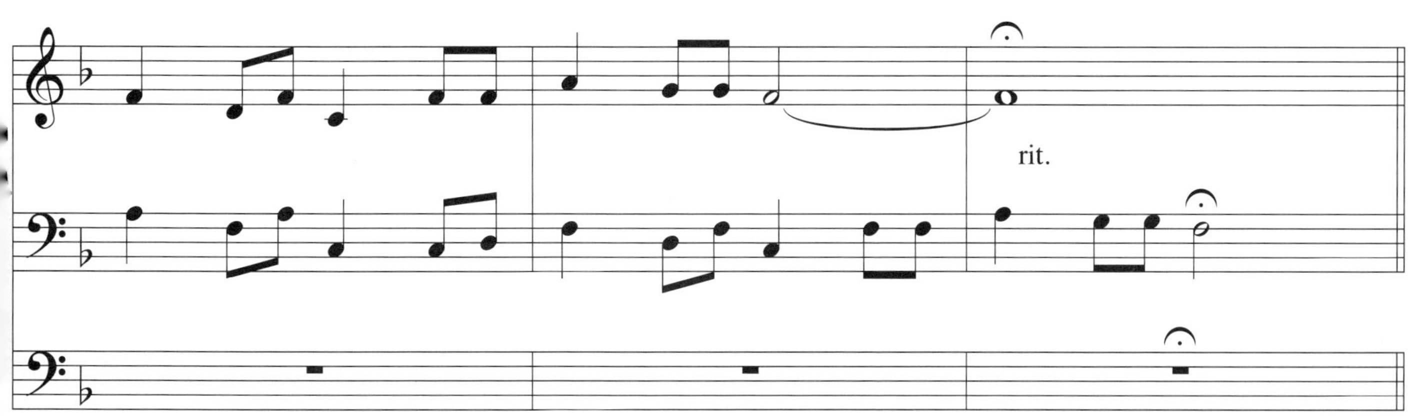

Sw. (Strings 8' & 4')
Gt.
Sw.

Gt.
Sw.
Sw.
rit.
March-like
Sw. (Flute 4', 2' & 1')
a tempo
Gt. (Princiapl 8' & 4')
detatched
Principal 8'

Gt.
Gt.
Sw.
Full organ
Gt.

add crescendo

rit.

a tempo

rit.

8va

The Battle of Jericho

Sw. Strings 8' & 4'
Gt. Bourdon 8' & 4'
Ped. Bourdon 16' & 8'

Spiritual
Arranged by Terry L. Baldridge

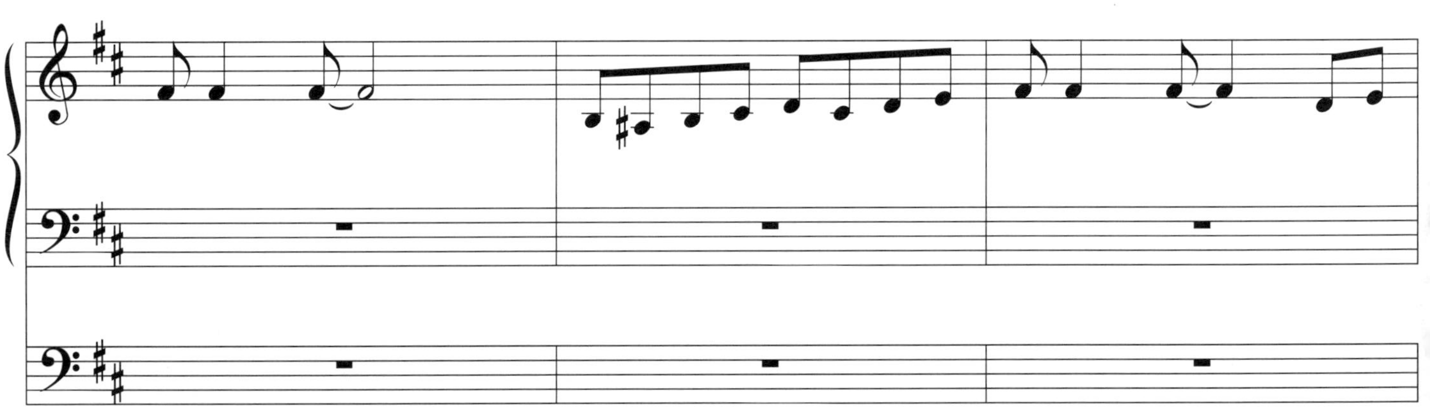

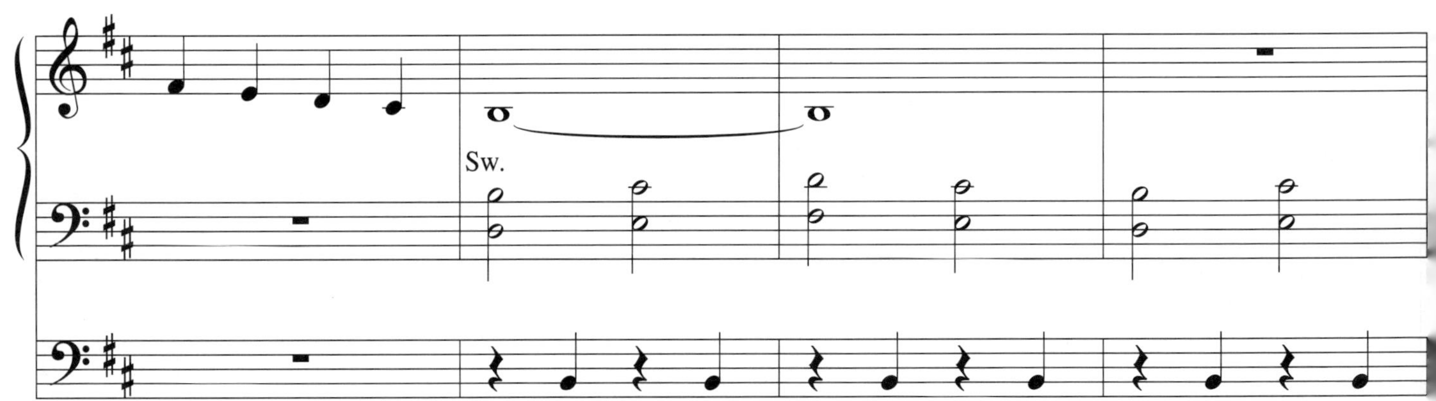

Gt.
rit.
Gt.

rit.
Principal 16' & 8'
rit.
slowly

Arise, My Soul, Arise

LENOX

Sw. Full
Gt. Full
Ped. Full

LEWIS EDSON
Arranged by Terry L. Baldridge

Gt. (Principal 8')
Sw. (Strings 8' & 4')
Bourdon 16' & 8'

Sw.
rit.
(Full Organ)
Gt.

(add solo reeds)

molto rit.

Jacob's Ladder

Sw. Strings 8' & 4'
Gt. Chimes
Ped. Bourdon 16' & 8'

Spiritual
Arranged by Terry L. Baldridge

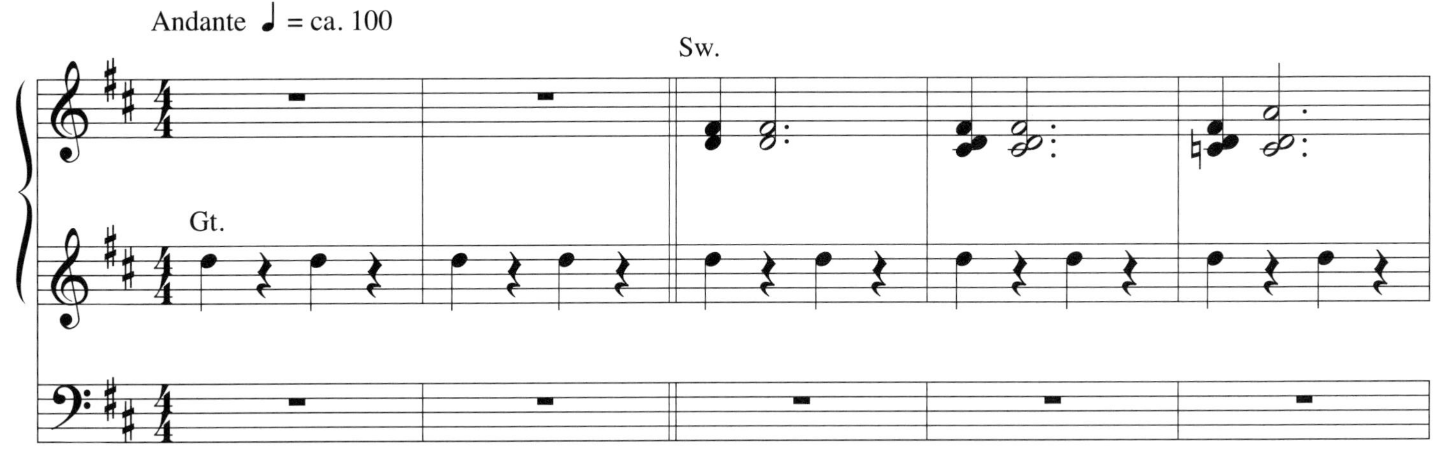

Bourdon 8' & 4'
Gt.

Sw.
Gt. Chimes

I Have Decided to Follow Jesus

ASSAM

Sw. String Celeste
Gt. Bourdon 8', Principal
Ped. Bourdon 16' & 8'

Folk Melody from India
Arranged by Terry L. Baldridge

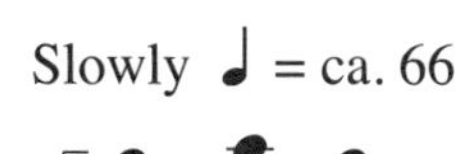

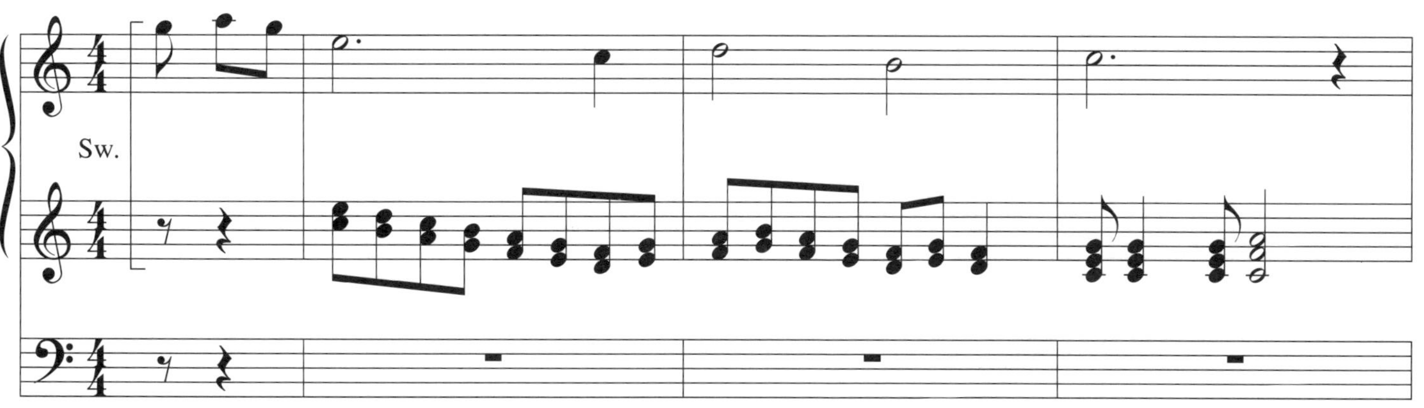

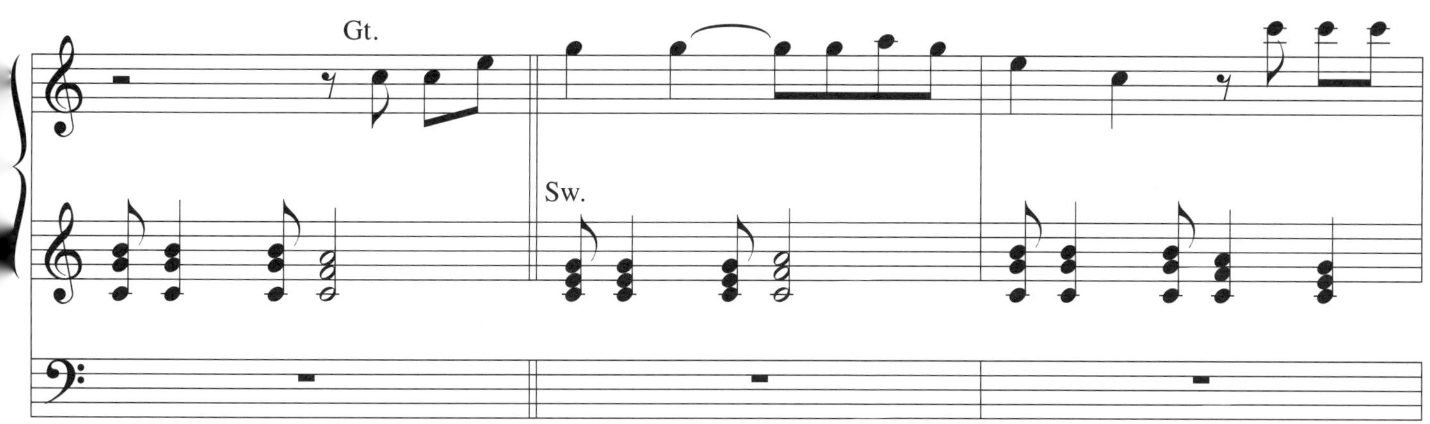

Maestoso
Full organ
Gt.

Thine Is the Glory

RIGAUDON/MACCABEUS

Sw. Full
Gt. Full
Ped. Full

Ragaudon from *"Idoménée"* (1712) by ANDRE CAMPRA
Maccabeus from *"Judas Maccabeus"* (1747) by G. F. HANDEL
Arranged by Terry L. Baldridge

Sw.
Gt.

Sw.
Gt.

cresc.
ff
rit.

Eternal Life

ETERNAL LIFE

Sw. Flutes 8', 4' & 2 2/3'
Gt. Bourdon 8' & 4'
Ped. Bourdon 16' & 8'

OLIVE DUNGAN
Arranged by Terry L. Baldridge

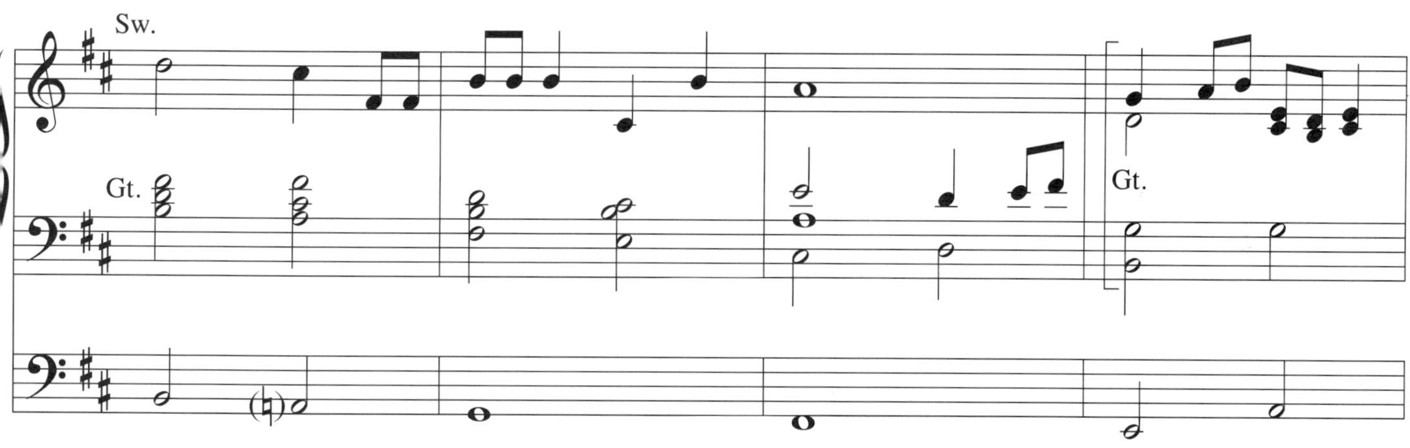

add Principal 8' & 4'
Gt.
cresc.
cresc.
(Full)

Immortal, Invisible

JOANNA

Sw. Strings 8' & 4'
Gt. Principal 8' & 4'
Ped. Bourdon 16' & 8'

Welsh Hymn Tune
Arranged by Terry L. Baldridge

Maestoso ♩ = ca. 120

rit.
Sw.
Andante
Gt. (Principal 8')

Sw.
Gt.
Sw.
rit.
Sw. (Full)
Allegro
Gt. (Principal 8' & 4', Bourdon 8' & 4')
Gt. to Pedal, Bourdon 16' & 8', Principal 8' & 4'

ten.
Gradually add crescendo
Gt.
Majestic
broaden
Melody
add solo reeds

'Tis So Sweet to Trust in Jesus

TRUST IN JESUS

Sw. String Celeste 8'
Gt. Bourdon 8' & 4'
Ped. Bourdon 16' & 8'

WILLIAM J. KIRKPATRICK
Arranged by Terry L. Baldridge

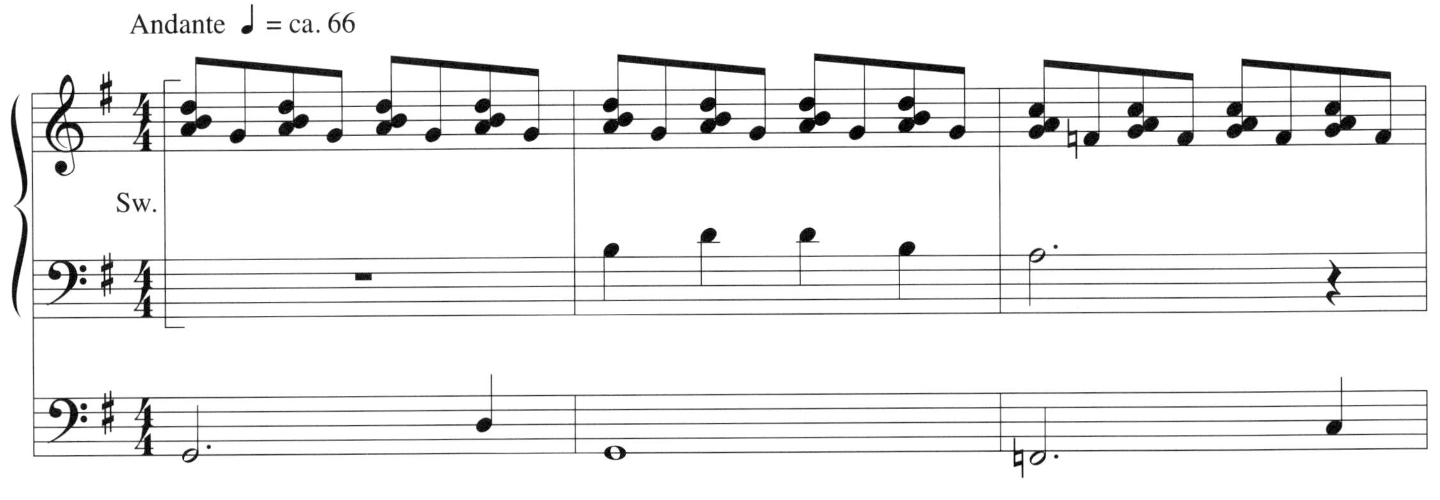

Sw.

rit.
Gt.
freely
Sw.

Gt.
Sw.
rit.

Holy, Holy, Holy, Lord God Almighty

NICAEA

Sw. Chimes
Gt. Bourdon 8' & 4'
Ped. Bourdon 16' & 8'

JOHN B. DYKES
Arranged by Terry L. Baldridge

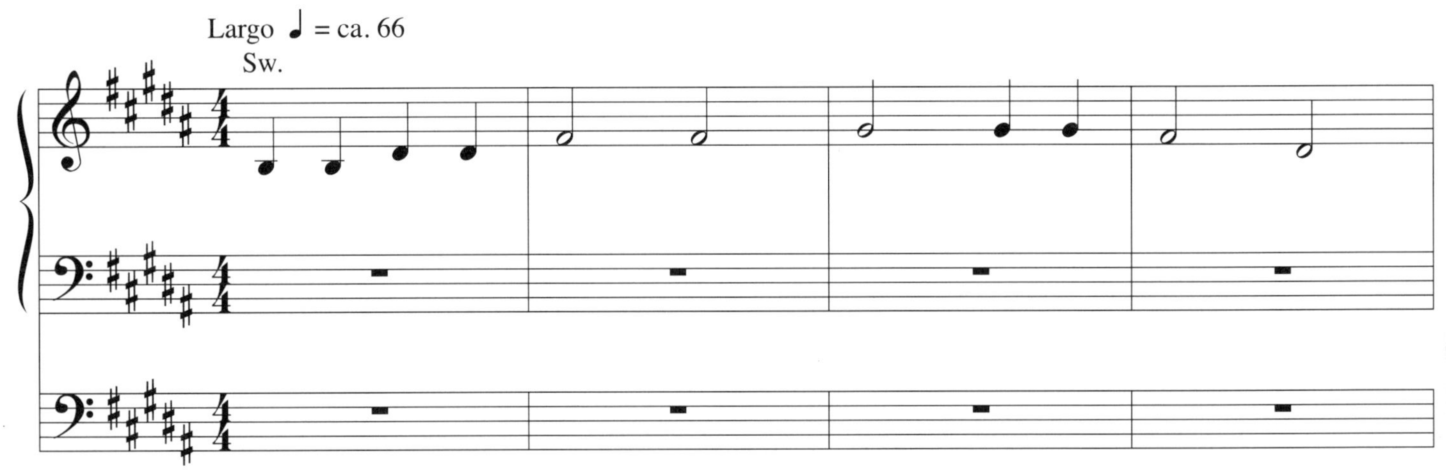

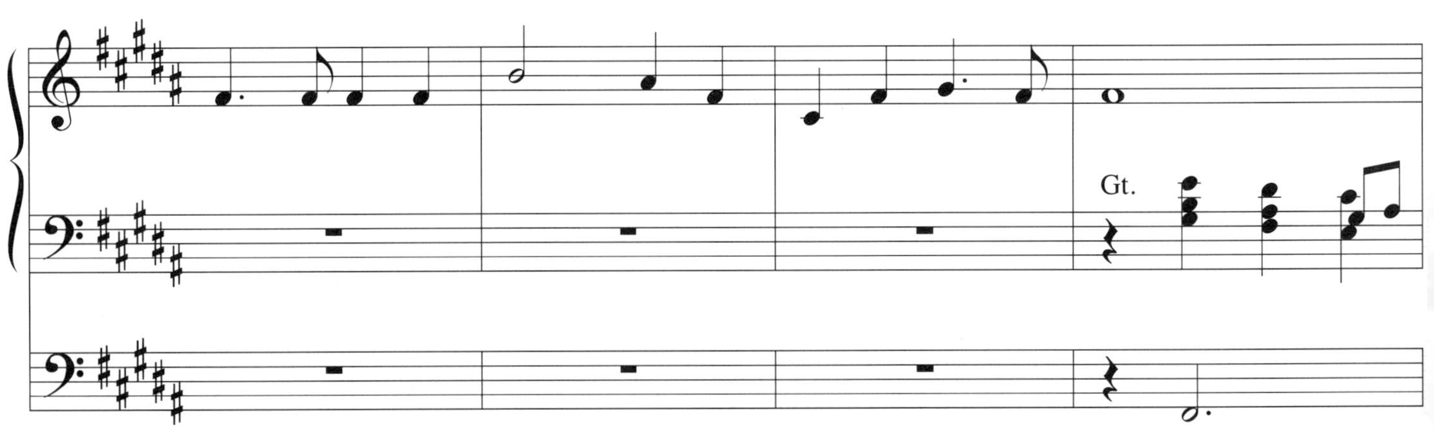

Gt.

rit.
Full organ

Worship the King

with

O Come, Let Us Adore Him

Sw. Full
Gt. Full
Ped. Full

BILLY SMILEY and BILL GEORGE
Arranged by Terry L. Baldridge

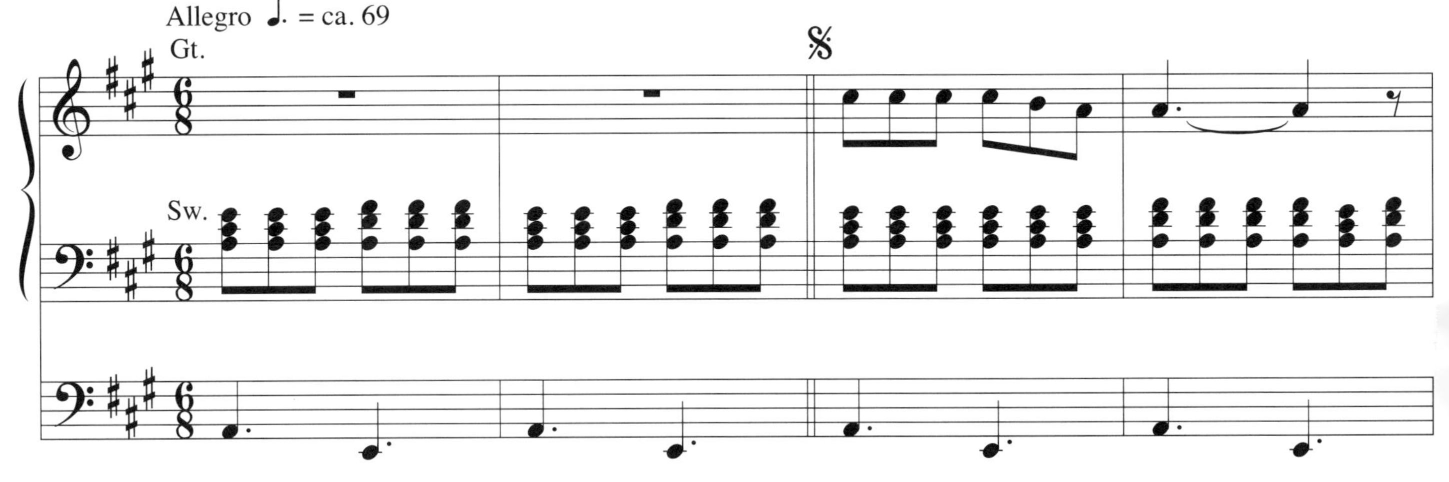

2nd time to Coda
Sw.

*Music attr. to John F. Wade. Arr. © 1999 by Lillenas Publishing Company (SESAC) All rights reserved. Administered by The Copyright Company, 40 Music Square East, Nashville, TN 372

add crescendo
Gt.

For Harlan Plunkett

Trumpet Tune in F

Sw. Trumpet 8'
Gt. Princiapl 8' & 4', Bourdon 8' & 4'
Gt. to Ped.
Ped. Bourdon 16' & 8', Principal 8' & 4'

TERRY L. BALDRIDGE

Maestoso ♩ = ca. 80

(♭)
(♭)
Sw.
Gt.
Repeat on Gt.
Gt.

(♭)
(♭)

Sw.
Gt.

Full organ on repeat
rit. last time